TOWNSHIP OF UNION
FREE PUBLIC LIBRARY

D1229708

HEINEMANN
STATE STUDIES

People of
New Jersey

Mark Stewart

Heinemann Library
Chicago, Illinois

TOWNSHIP OF UNION
FREE PUBLIC LIBRARY

© 2004 Heinemann Library
a division of Reed Elsevier Inc.
Chicago, Illinois

Customer Service 888-454-2279

Visit our website at www.heinemannlibrary.com

All rights reserved. No part of this publication
may be reproduced or transmitted in any form or
by any means, electronic or mechanical, including
photocopying, recording, taping, or any
information storage and retrieval system, without
permission in writing from the publisher.

Designed by Heinemann Library
Page layout by Wilkinson Design
Printed and bound in the United States by
  Lake Book Manufacturing, Inc.

08 07 06 05 04
10 9 8 7 6 5 4 3 2 1

**Library of Congress
Cataloging-in-Publication Data**

Stewart, Mark, 1960-
  People of New Jersey / Mark Stewart.
    p. cm. -- (State studies)
Summary: Examines the diversity of peoples who
inhabit New Jersey, including Native Americans
and immigrants from many lands.
Includes bibliographical references and index.
  ISBN 1-4034-0675-8 (HC library binding) -- ISBN
1-4034-2686-4 (PB) 1. Ethnology--New Jersey--
Juvenile literature. 2. Minorities--New Jersey--Juve-
nile literature. 3. Immigrants--New Jersey--Juvenile
literature. 4. New Jersey--Population--Juvenile literature. 5. New Jersey--History--Juvenile literature. 6.
New Jersey--Ethnic relations--Juvenile literature. [1.
Ethnology--New Jersey. 2. New Jersey--Population.
3. Minorities--New Jersey. 4. Immigrants--New
Jersey.] I. Title. II. Series. F145.A1S75 2003
  974.9--dc21

2003010355

Acknowledgments

The author and publishers are grateful to the
following for permission to reproduce copyright
material:

Cover photographs by (main) Ric Dean/Corbis;
(row, T-B) Mike Derer/AP WideWorld, Underwood
& Underwood/Corbis, Hector Emmanuel/
Heinemann Library, Corbis

Title page (L-R) Mitchell Gerber/Corbis,
Underwood & Underwood/Corbis, AP WideWorld
Photos; contents page (L-R) James L. Amos/Corbis,
Mike Derer/AP WideWorld; p. 4 Richard T. Nowitz/
Corbis; p. 9 Robert Griffin; pp. 10, 12, 20, 25, 26,
33, 40b Bettmann/Corbis; pp. 11, 14, 19, 21 The
Granger Collection, New York; pp. 13,Library of
Congress; p 16 The Granger Collection; p. 15
James L. Amos/Corbis; p. 17 North Wind Picture
Archives; p. 22 Bob Krist/Corbis; p. 23 Underwood
& Underwood/Corbis; pp. 24, 27, 29 Hector
Emmanuel/Heinemann Library; p. 28 Kelly-Mooney
Photography/Corbis; p. 30 NewsCom; p. 31
Mitchell Gerber/Corbis; p. 32 AP WideWorld
Photos; pp. 34, 44 Corbis; pp. 35, 43t AFP/Corbis;
p. 36 Jacques M. Chenet/Corbis; p. 37 Ansel
Adams Publishing Rights Trust/Corbis; p. 38t
Ronald Siemoneit /Corbis SYGMA; p. 38b Michael
Conroy/AP Wide World Photos; p. 39 Pacha/
Corbis; p. 40t Hulton-Deutsch Collection/Corbis;
p. 41 Mike Derer/AP WideWorld; p. 42 Rufus F.
Folkks/Corbis; p. 43b Robert Eric/Corbis SYGMA

Photo research by John Klein

Special thanks to to expert reader Chad
Leinaweaver, the Director for the Library at The
New Jersey Historical Society, for his help in the
preparation of this book.

Every effort has been made to contact copyright
holders of any material reproduced in this book.
Any omissions will be rectified in subsequent
printings if notice is given to the publisher.

$18.95

JRNJ
917.49
STE
c.2

Some words are shown in bold, **like this.**
You can find out what they mean by looking
in the glossary.

Contents

New Jersey's People

Throughout its history, New Jersey has opened its arms to the world. For centuries it has offered hope, shelter, and opportunity to millions of people. New Jersey's unique combination of **natural resources, fertile** land, and long coastline has served its people well in both good times and bad. The story of the state is best told through the stories of the people who lived there in the past and who live there now.

New Jersey is the fifth smallest state in the United States. Only Connecticut, Delaware, Hawaii, and Rhode Island are smaller. But New Jersey is the ninth largest state in population. New Jersey's small size and large population make the state's population **density** the largest in the United States.

THE 2000 CENSUS

According to the 2000 **census,** 8,414,350 people live in New Jersey. This is an increase of about nine percent since 1990, when 7,747,750 people lived in the state.

According to the 2000 Census, the population density in New Jersey is 1,134.4 residents per square mile. Some counties are more densely populated than others.

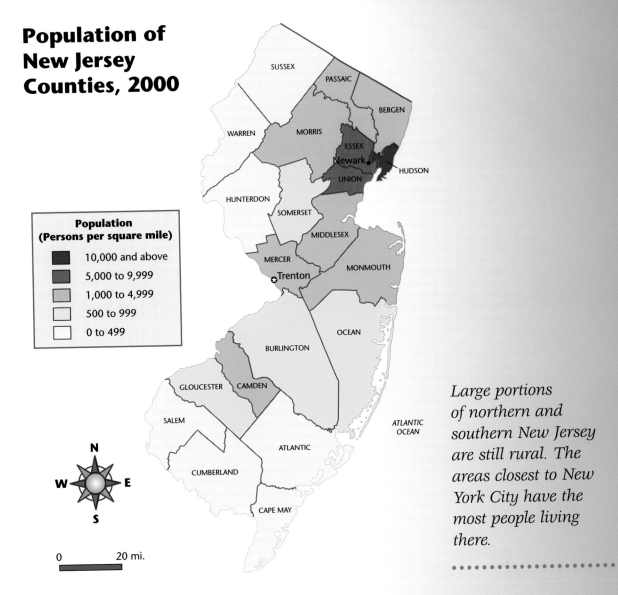

Population of New Jersey Counties, 2000

**Population
(Persons per square mile)**

- 10,000 and above
- 5,000 to 9,999
- 1,000 to 4,999
- 500 to 999
- 0 to 499

Large portions of northern and southern New Jersey are still rural. The areas closest to New York City have the most people living there.

New Jersey has seven cities with a population of 75,000 or more. Newark is the largest city, with nearly 274,000 people. The other cities and **municipalities** with a population of more than 75,000 are Jersey City, Paterson, Elizabeth, Trenton, Camden, Clifton, Edison Township, Hamilton Township, Woodbridge Township, and Dover Township.

WHERE PEOPLE LIVE IN NEW JERSEY

Most people in New Jersey live in **urban** areas. According to the 2000 census, about 94 percent of New Jersey' people live in urban areas and only 6 percent live in **rural** areas. That means that out of every 100 people who live in New Jersey, 94 live in the state's villages, towns, and cities.

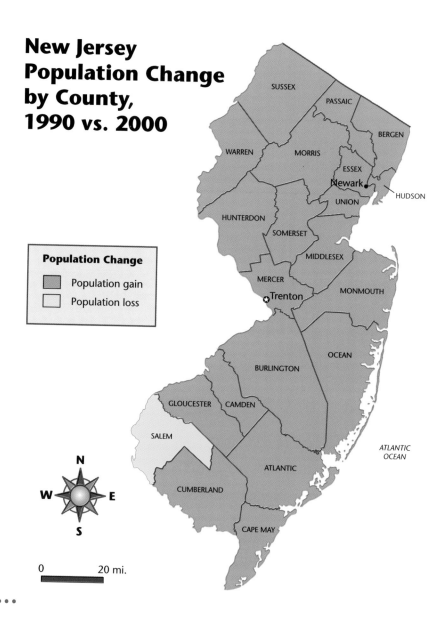

New Jersey Population Change by County, 1990 vs. 2000

Population Change

Population gain

Population loss

SUSSEX

PASSAIC

BERGEN

WARREN

MORRIS

ESSEX

Newark

HUDSON

UNION

HUNTERDON

SOMERSET

MIDDLESEX

MERCER

Trenton

MONMOUTH

OCEAN

BURLINGTON

GLOUCESTER

CAMDEN

SALEM

ATLANTIC OCEAN

N

W

E

S

ATLANTIC

CUMBERLAND

CAPE MAY

0   20 mi.

Between 1990 and 2000, only one county in New Jersey did not gain more residents.

Many people in New Jersey live in the state's nine **metropolitan** areas. These areas include Atlantic-Cape May, Bergen-Passaic, Jersey City, Middlesex-Somerset-Hunterdon, Monmouth-Ocean, Newark, Philadelphia (Pennsylvania), Trenton, and Vineland-Millevile-Bridgeton.

In the northern part of New Jersey, six metropolitan areas combined with four metropolitan areas in New York and five in Connecticut make up an area known as the New York–Northern New Jersey–Long Island Consolidated Metropolitan Statistical Area. About 21 million people live there.

A DIVERSE STATE

People in New Jersey represent different races and **ethnic** groups. About 73 percent of New Jerseyans are Caucasian, and about 14 percent are African American. Asians make up about 6 percent of New Jersey's population. Other peoples, such as Native Americans, make up a small percentage of New Jersey's entire population.

There is a big difference in population among New Jersey's ten largest cities. Newark has over four times as many people as Union City.

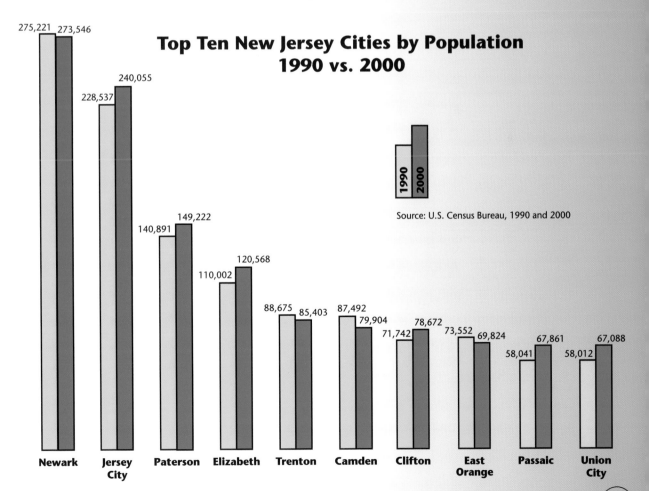

**Top Ten New Jersey Cities by Population
1990 vs. 2000**

1990
2000

Source: U.S. Census Bureau, 1990 and 2000

275,221 273,546 — Newark
228,537 240,055 — Jersey City
140,891 149,222 — Paterson
110,002 120,568 — Elizabeth
88,675 85,403 — Trenton
87,492 79,904 — Camden
71,742 78,672 — Clifton
73,552 69,824 — East Orange
58,041 67,861 — Passaic
58,012 67,088 — Union City

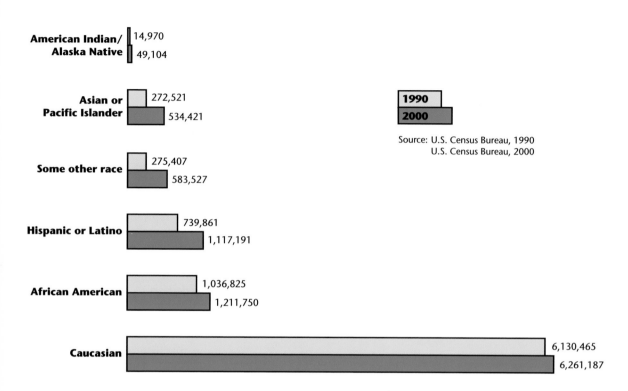

New Jersey's Demographics: 1990 vs. 2000

American Indian/ Alaska Native
14,970
49,104

Asian or Pacific Islander
272,521
534,421

Some other race
275,407
583,527

Hispanic or Latino
739,861
1,117,191

African American
1,036,825
1,211,750

Caucasian
6,130,465
6,261,187

1990
2000

Source: U.S. Census Bureau, 1990
U.S. Census Bureau, 2000

*Between 1990 and 2000, New Jersey became more **diverse.** People of all races live in New Jersey.*

About 13 percent of New Jersey's people are of Hispanic **descent.** Other **ethnic** groups in New Jersey include people of Italian, Irish, German, and British descent.

A STATE OF CONTRASTS

New Jersey is a state of contrasts. It has all types of communities: **urban, suburban,** and **rural.** New Jersey is home to people of great wealth and great poverty. Its residents have a variety of **cultural** backgrounds. The state is home to historical figures and people who are just now becoming famous. But no matter where people live or who they are, they all call New Jersey "home."

First People and Early Settlers

The first people to come to what is now the United States were part of a group who **migrated** from Asia to North America, beginning about 40,000 years ago. These people traveled over a land bridge that then connected Asia to what is now Alaska. Today, a body of water called the Bering Strait separates these places. About 12,000 years ago, groups of these people began arriving in what is now New Jersey.

These ancient peoples were the **ancestors** of the Native Americans who lived in the state when the first white people arrived in the 1600s. They called themselves *Lenape*, which means "original people." The Lenape were a part of the

Europeans called the Lenape the "Delaware Indians" because they lived near the Delaware River.

Algonquin language group whose nations stretched up and down the Atlantic coast. The Lenape were known for their wisdom and respected for their peaceful ways. Because of their reputation for being fair and just, Lenape leaders were often called upon to settle disputes among other Algonquian tribes.

The native people of New Jersey saw the first Europeans in 1524, when explorer Giovanni da Verrazano sailed up the Atlantic Coast past several Lenape settlements. Verrazano wrote of native people who came aboard his ship. These people are believed to have been the Lenape.

A Century of Tears

During the first 100 years of contact with European settlers, diseases carried by white settlers destroyed New Jersey's native peoples. By the mid-1700s, less than a thousand Lenape were left, due mostly to diseases such as smallpox. In 1758, the state's remaining Native Americans signed a **treaty** agreeing to move to Brotherton, called Indian Mills today, in the Pine Barrens. This is believed to be the country's first Native American **reservation.** Unable to make a living here, the entire tribe moved north to New York state and eventually further north and west. Although several thousand New Jerseyans today describe themselves as having Native American **ancestors,** it is doubtful that more than a few are **descended** from the state's native peoples.

The Lenape most likely came in contact with white people again in what is now Sandy Hook Bay. There in 1609, explorer Henry Hudson anchored his ship, the *Half Moon*. Hudson's men probably came ashore to search for water and food. It is possible they encountered some of the native people who had earlier waved to them from shore. Hudson sailed on to Newark Bay, then up the river that later was named for him, the Hudson River.

This painting shows the discovery of the Hudson River by Henry Hudson sailing the Half Moon *in 1609.*

Although Dutch trappers and fur traders explored New Jersey in the 1620s, the first Europeans to settle here did not come until about ten years later. They built their homes on land that the Dutchman Michael Pauw bought in 1630. He named it Pavonia, which means "land of the Peacock." It lay across the harbor from the Dutch settlement of New Amsterdam, near the present-day cities of Jersey City and Hoboken. The houses in Pavonia were the first on the New Jersey side of the Hudson River.

The first settlers found cornfields and piles of oyster shells, which showed that the Lenape used this area as a summer residence. That made no difference to the Dutch, who did not recognize the Native Americans' claim to the land.

The Lenape tried to live in peace with the settlers, but in 1643, a group of soldiers from the **fort** in New Amsterdam **massacred** 80 Lenape while they were sleeping. This incident forever changed the relationship between New Jersey's white settlers and the Native Americans. Contact between the two groups was rare, but when it did occur, the results were often deadly for both sides. Raids took the lives of many settlers, while European diseases killed many Native Americans.

COLONIAL LIFE IN NEW JERSEY

In 1660, New Amsterdam's governor, Peter Stuyvesant, approved the establishment of a **fortified** town, which he named Bergen. A year later, New Jersey had its first school, first church, and first seat of government. Little changed in 1664 when England took over the **colony,** other than giving it a new name in honor of James, the Duke of York. When James gave this territory to his friends, John Berkeley and George Carteret, they sent Carteret's relative, Philip Carteret, to govern it. George Carteret was the governor of the Isle

*When Stuyvesant arrived in New Amsterdam, he told the **colonists,** "I shall govern you as a father his children."*

This house was built by David des Marest in 1678. It was moved from New Milford to a park in Hackensack in the 1950s.

of Jersey in England, and the land was renamed New Jersey in his honor.

The Dutch tried to regain this territory in 1673. Finally, a **treaty** between England and Holland placed what is now New Jersey firmly in British hands.

The Dutch settlers, living under British rule, moved further inland into New Jersey. They journeyed up the Hackensack and Raritan Rivers, where they started settlements that would remain Dutch-speaking for one hundred years or more.

Other groups besides the Dutch had also settled in New Jersey. A few of the British officers stationed in the colony chose to stay after they retired. They purchased large pieces of land and established what are now the towns of Harrison, Kearny, and Secaucus. People from Finland and Sweden, sailing around New Jersey's southern tip, began settlements on the eastern shore of the Delaware River.

Despite the heavy Dutch presence to the north, it was a Frenchman, David des Marest, who founded the first permanent town along the Hackensack River, in what is today New Milford. However, the nearby town of Hackensack quickly grew larger. Hackensack's harbor was deep enough to dock ocean-going vessels, and the surrounding land was very **fertile. Trade** and farming grew in this area. To the south, Dutch settlers traveled up the Raritan River to found the town of New Brunswick.

Ironworkers were the most important workers in the colonies. They made and repaired tools for other workers, repaired guns, and provided the tools people needed to build their homes.

In the central part of the state, near the Atlantic Ocean, the inland towns of Middletown, Shrewsbury, and Freehold began to **thrive.** Along the coast, where storms often washed right over the long, narrow strip of land that ran south from Sandy Hook, **colonists** established few permanent settlements. Toms River was an exception. Harvesting salt from the seawater helped to make it an important town. People used salt to preserve meat, as they had no means of refrigeration to keep it fresh.

INDUSTRY IN THE COLONY

The most important **industry** during the early years of the New Jersey colony was ironworking. Around 1700, settlers discovered deposits of iron **ore** in Succasunna. They processed the ore in the nearby town of Hanover before it was taken onto British ships headed for England. There was enough iron ore in the ground to help make other towns, including

Dover, Hibernia, Ringwood, and Rockaway, good places for iron mills.

In the southwestern part of the colony, along the Delaware River, glassblowing became an important industry. In 1739, Caspar Wistar, a Philadelphia buttonmaker, built a glass factory in Salem City. He hired skilled glassblowers from Europe and hired local people as **apprentices.** The seven Stanger brothers worked for him for many years before starting a factory of their own in the 1770s, in nearby Glassboro. This part of New Jersey would one day become one of the most well-known glassblowing centers in the world.

Today, Glassboro has a museum dedicated to the history of glassmaking. There you can watch demonstrations and see the final products.

QUAKERS

Southern New Jersey also became home to a large concentration of Quakers. These peace-loving people had been **persecuted** in England for their religious beliefs. However, they found religious freedom in New Jersey. One of the religion's leaders, John Woolman, wrote about the **inhumanity** of slavery. As in all the **colonies,** slavery was legal in New Jersey during the 1700s. Woolman's writings convinced his fellow Quakers to become active in the antislavery cause. Thanks in large part to the Quakers, in the 1800s southern New Jersey became an important stop on the Underground Railroad, which was a network of safe houses and hiding places that led slaves north to freedom.

Great Scot!

In 1768, the College of New Jersey hired John Witherspoon of Scotland to head the school. Leaving his homeland behind, Witherspoon took his work seriously, hiring the best teachers, and attracting the finest students from the thirteen colonies. In no time, the school—later renamed Princeton—became known both for the tremendous education its graduates received and the leadership of its president. Witherspoon was so highly regarded that he was chosen to be one of the signers of the Declaration of Independence.

Immigration Changes New Jersey

By the start of the American Revolution (1775–1783), around 100,000 people lived in the New Jersey colony. Although they could trace their roots back to more than a dozen different countries, New Jerseyans were all ruled by the British. However, they did not feel that they were being treated fairly by Britain. Much of the lumber, iron, and food they produced left the colony on ships bound for England. In return they received finished goods, such as clothing, tools, and furniture. Many New Jerseyans believed they would be better off producing these things themselves.

*General George Washington and the **Continental Army** spent almost half of the American Revolution (1775–1783) in New Jersey.*

Trade Routes

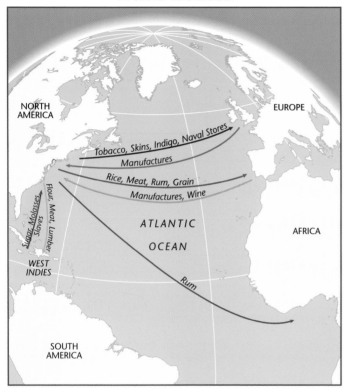

New Jersey was in a good position for receiving goods shipped from other countries. Products produced in the colonies often left through New Jersey ports, too.

In the mid-1700s, the British government began taxing the American **colonists** to pay off **debts** from a long war it fought with France. Many colonists became angry. The colonists believed that the British government did not have the right to tax them because the colonists were not represented in **Parliament.** The British government refused to listen to the colonists' complaints. As a result, the colonists believed that they should no longer be part of Britain. They declared their **independence,** and the American Revolution began. Many, but not all, New Jersey colonists supported the cause.

General George Washington of Virginia was named the leader of the **Continental Army.** Because Britain had firm control of New York and Philadelphia, Washington had to keep New Jersey out of the enemy's hands. Washington's Continental Army fought many battles on New Jersey's soil. On several occasions, the New Jersey **militia** helped the Continental Army in their fight against the British.

After the American colonists won the war in 1781, the thirteen colonies became the first thirteen states of the United States. The population of the state of New Jersey nearly doubled in the ten years after the war. Many people came to New Jersey because of the **fertile** land

and the factories that were there. Many people who worked in skilled **trades,** such as ironworkers, glass-blowers, machinists, and engineers, streamed into New Jersey from Britain and what is now Germany.

The Crossroads

Many small and major battles of the American Revolution were fought in New Jersey. In fact, more battles were fought in New Jersey than anywhere else, earning the state the nickname Crossroads of the American Revolution.

IMMIGRANTS HELP THE STATE GROW

In the 1790s, a group of New Yorkers started the city of Paterson. It was the first planned **industrial** town in the United States. Built along the Passaic River, the waterpower was used to provide energy to the many factories in Paterson. People began arriving in Paterson because of the work, housing, and shopping there. Paterson

Paterson was established as a way to reduce the colonists' dependence on British goods. New industries created the products the people needed to survive.

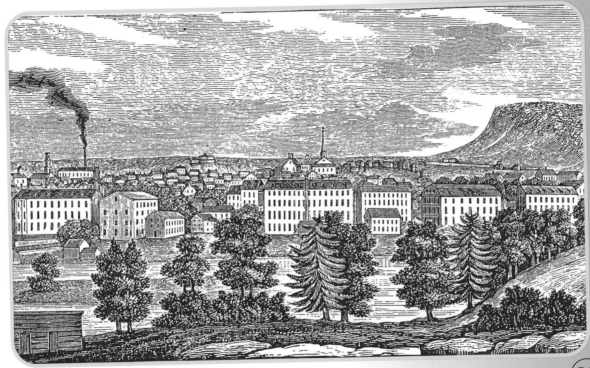

was the first of a string of New Jersey river towns to grow in the early 1800s. Some were located on major rivers, while others grew in a line stretching between New York and Philadelphia.

To move goods east to New York City and west to Philadelphia, New Jersey built a system of **canals** and railroads during the 1800s. The job opportunities for this project brought a wave of **immigrants** to New Jersey from Ireland. In the mid-1800s, a disease destroyed Ireland's potato crop, causing many people there to suffer from **famine.** There were few jobs available in Ireland, and everyday life was a struggle.

In the 1840s, large numbers of Germans immigrated to New Jersey. Most of these immigrants were fleeing from wars at home. They had tried to gain the freedoms Americans enjoyed. When they were unsuccessful, they decided it was better to start a new life in the United States. Most of the German immigrants were well-educated and anxious to be involved in their community. Those who

This is an example of canal money. It was issued by New Jersey in 1841 because the United States government would not provide money to build the canals.

New immigrants often faced an uncertain future. Many came to New Jersey with no money, no job, and no place to live.

settled in New Jersey gave the state a big boost in science, education, and **industry.** Also among this group were many Jews who were fleeing religious **persecution** at home.

By the 1870s, New Jersey was also getting a trickle of immigrants from Eastern Europe, from countries such as Bulgaria, Hungary, Poland, Romania, and Russia. Over the next 50 years, this trickle grew larger, and included immigrants from Italy, Spain, Greece, and Portugal. The people who came to New Jersey during this time were mostly poor and uneducated. Bad harvests and other hardships drove people from their farms. They had no choice but to begin again wherever they could.

Many new **immigrants** were hungry, homeless, and hopeless. They were not able to cope with life in a big city like New York but were too poor to journey to the American West. They chose to settle in New Jersey, a place that offered open spaces and decent wages.

During the years following the Civil War (1861–1865), **industry** in New Jersey was booming and in desperate need of people willing to work hard. Many people moved for jobs to the growing cities in New Jersey. With more people arriving to fill these jobs, the demand for food increased each year. This meant that New Jersey needed farmers, too.

Help Wanted

One of history's most successful farming experiments began in 1861. At that time Charles Landis, a Philadelphia attorney, began hiring Italian farmers to farm the sandy soil of his property in the Pine Barrens. The Italians were world-famous for working with difficult soil. Soon, they turned land that had long

been considered not **fertile** into a successful piece of real estate. Vineland, as the town was called, was a big success. As word spread, more landowners began looking for Italian farmers. They actually advertised in Italy, posting notices that said how much New Jersey's **climate** was like their own.

Those immigrants who were looking for immediate work headed for cities like Camden, Elizabeth, Hoboken, Jersey City, Newark, Paterson, and Trenton. There they found factories looking for cheap labor, as well as **ethnic** neighborhoods where they could hear and speak their own language and eat familiar foods. Those immigrants who were looking for better pay took riskier, backbreaking work at the brickworks along the Raritan River, the mines in the New Jersey Highlands around Dover, or in the oil refineries in Bayonne.

Immigrants often had to take difficult jobs, such as laying pipeline. It took many hours of hard labor to lay 205,000 miles of oil pipelines across the country.

New immigrants in the late 1800s and early 1900s found work taking care of the gardens of wealthy families and working the flower farms that supplied New York City's grand hotels, restaurants, and private homes. In the summer and fall, many immigrant families would **migrate** to the farms of southern New Jersey to harvest cranberries, blueberries, and other seasonal crops. It was not easy work, but it provided a break from the heat of the more **urban** settings.

In the early 1900s, thousands of African Americans from the South **migrated** to the North. They were looking to escape **racism** in the South and to find better job opportunities in the North. Many settled in New Jersey's cities as well as in other northern cities. This huge movement of people became known as the **Great Migration.**

Among New Jersey's permanent residents at the turn of the century were large numbers of Jewish **immigrants** from Russia. The Jews in Russia had been **persecuted** for their religion. Their homes had been burned, their possessions taken, and their relatives killed by the country's rulers. Those who survived made the long, dangerous journey to the United States, and attempted to recreate a bit of their homeland. They started

Many immigrants start small businesses in their neighborhoods. This helps to build a sense of community among the people who live in the area.

several communities, including the village of Woodbine and the towns of Alliance, Brotmanville, Carmel, Norma, and Rosenhayn.

In all, more than half a million immigrants settled in New Jersey in the years before World War I (1914–1918). In the early part of the 1900s, a quarter of New Jersey's residents had been born overseas.

Gateway to America

Only 1,000 feet from the docks of Jersey City stood Ellis Island, where officials processed millions of immigrants from the 1890s to the 1950s. Many of these newcomers actually set foot in New Jersey first. Ferries took them to Jersey City and Hoboken, where trains waited to bring them to new lives and new jobs in the American South and West. Others moved across the river to New York City. And of course, tens of thousands put down roots or joined family and friends in New Jersey. Although people always thought of Ellis Island and the Statue of Liberty as belonging to New York, in the 1990s, a court ruled that these two historic landmarks actually lie in New Jersey waters.

At Work and On the Move

Immigration laws passed during the 1920s greatly reduced the number of people entering the United States from overseas. However, of those who were allowed to immigrate between the 1920s and 1960s, many came to New Jersey. As with past generations of new New Jerseyans, the state's many economic opportunities attracted them. Opportunities existed in areas such as research, education, medicine, and technology.

On December 8, 1930, Ford Motor Company opened a plant in Edgewater, New Jersey. It was the largest of its kind in the United States.

In recent decades, New Jersey has welcomed yet another wave of **immigrants.** Although every country in the world is represented in

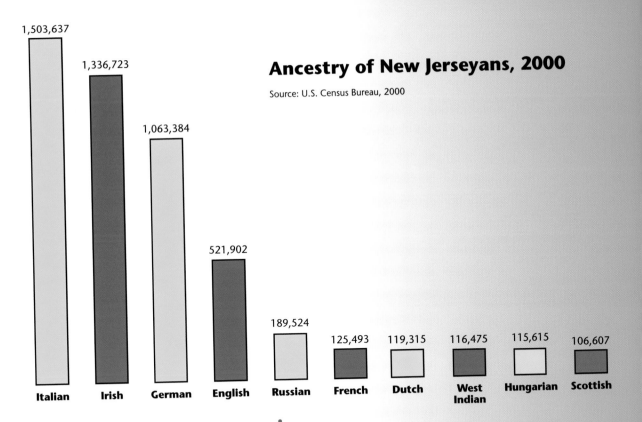

Ancestry of New Jerseyans, 2000

Source: U.S. Census Bureau, 2000

Italian	Irish	German	English	Russian	French	Dutch	West Indian	Hungarian	Scottish
1,503,637	1,336,723	1,063,384	521,902	189,524	125,493	119,315	116,475	115,615	106,607

*Many people of New Jersey can trace their family roots back to different countries. People of Italian, Irish, German, and English **descent** make up the largest groups.*

this group, most of the people came from countries in Latin America and Asia. Also, a large number of people from Italy continue to immigrate to New Jersey. In fact, people tracing their **heritage** back to Italy now make up the largest single **ethnic** group in the state.

For more than a century, most immigrants to the United States had settled in larger cities. There,

Ethnic neighborhoods often look very similar to neighborhoods in the native countries that immigrants came from.

Several dancers are performing at the Cultural Festival of India in Middlesex County, New Jersey.

newcomers found **ethnic** neighborhoods that offered familiar food and faces, a place to live, and a paying job. In recent years, however, New Jersey has changed that picture. People from all over the world have put down roots in the state's more than 500 small towns and cities. Researchers expect this trend to continue all over the United States, with newcomers skipping over large **urban** areas and settling in small towns and **suburbs.**

THE NEWEST IMMIGRANTS

New Jersey is now one of the most ethnically **diverse** places in the world. Officially, about 17.5 percent of the people in New Jersey are either foreign-born or first-generation Americans. Over 65 different languages are spoken in the state.

The fastest-growing group of New Jerseyans comes from India and its neighboring countries. From 1990 to 2000, the Asian-Indian population in New Jersey more than doubled. Other Asian communities—including Chinese, Filipino, and Korean—also saw huge gains. These groups are proud of their **heritage** and have found an interesting balance between their traditional **cultures** and the new American culture. Many of their children attend New Jersey public schools during the week, then take special classes on Saturdays to learn about the cultures of their parents and grandparents.

While New Jersey has always had a significant Hispanic population, it has grown and changed dramatically in recent years. A generation ago, the state's Hispanic population was mainly Puerto Rican and Cuban. Today, less than half of the state's Hispanic residents trace their roots back to these places. Officially, Puerto Ricans make up the largest Hispanic group in New Jersey, while Cubans now rank fourth behind Mexicans and people from the Dominican Republic. People from Ecuador and Colombia also have moved to New Jersey in large numbers. Many of these people

Immigrants also come to New Jersey because of its strong economy, which makes it more likely they can find work.

have moved to New Jersey to escape poverty, violence, and political conflict in their countries.

Many of the newest **immigrants** to New Jersey have found work in the state's booming **industries.** With these jobs, they have been able to find housing in New Jersey's cities. They have also taken advantage of the educational opportunities that the state has to offer. These immigrants helped **revitalize** New Jersey's cities, which had seen their populations decline in the 1970s and 1980s. Places like Paterson and Passaic, for example, are today more than 50 percent Hispanic. They are once again home to **thriving,** vibrant communities.

Terror Affects New Jersey, Too

The terrorist attacks on New York City's World Trade Center on September 11, 2001, killed hundreds of New Jerseyans. Each day, tens of thousands of workers leave their homes in New Jersey and travel by bus, train, car, and boat to Manhattan's downtown financial district, and many were trapped in the World Trade Center

towers when they collapsed. The towns of eastern Monmouth County were particularly affected, as nearly 100 residents died in the attack. Despite its terrible losses, the people in this community sprang into action minutes after the attack. They sent doctors, food, and supplies into lower Manhattan on the same ferryboats that had brought their loved ones to work that morning. For many hours, this was the only safe way in and out of the stricken area.

New Jersey's Achievers

Addams, Charles (1912–1988), cartoonist. Charles Addams was born in Westfield, New Jersey. He began drawing cartoons during his high school years at Westfield High School, where he was the art editor for a school publication called the "Weather Vane." After studying at Grand Central School of Art in New York City, Addams began submitting cartoons to *The New Yorker Magazine*. He was hired at the magazine in 1940. Addams worked there until his death in 1988, drawing more than 1,300 cartoons during his career. Some of his cartoon characters became the basis for the popular 1960s television show *The Addams Family*.

Aldrin, Edwin "Buzz" (b. 1930), astronaut. Edwin "Buzz" Aldrin began his life in Montclair, New Jersey. He attended Montclair High School and graduated from the United States Military Academy at West Point, New York, in 1951. Aldrin received a doctorate of science in astronautics from Massachusetts Institute of Technology, in Cambridge. The National Aeronautics and Space Administration (NASA) named Aldrin as one of its third group of astronauts in 1963. In 1969, he served as the lunar module pilot in the first moon landing mission. Aldrin **resigned** from NASA in 1971.

Edwin "Buzz" Aldrin

Baraka, Amiri (b. 1934), poet. Amiri Baraka was born Everett LeRoi Jones in Newark, New Jersey, in 1934. He attended Rutgers University and earned a bachelor of arts degree from Howard University in 1954. An African-American **social activist,** Baraka has published many poems, plays, novels, and essays. He has lectured at several universities, including Rutgers, Yale, and the State University of New York. Baraka frequently lectures and reads from his works.

Basie, Count (1904–1984), musician. Count Basie was born William Basie in Red Bank, New Jersey. He received his first piano lessons from his mother, who was a pianist. Although at first Basie wanted to play the drums, a friend convinced him to take up the piano. Basie played in several jazz bands throughout the United States before forming his own band, The Count Basie Band, in 1936. Shortly after that, he and his band began recording. Basie is known for creating his own style of piano playing.

Judy Blume

Blume, Judy (b. 1938), author. Born in Elizabeth, New Jersey, Blume enjoyed making up stories as a young child. As an adult, she began writing books for children and adults, selling more than 75 million copies of her titles in all. Many of her novels deal with problems that young people face and are told from the young person's viewpoint. Many of her settings and characters are based on those she remembers as a child in New Jersey.

Bon Jovi, Jon (b. 1962), singer. John Francis Bongiovi was born in Perth Amboy, New Jersey. The young musician formed the group Bon Jovi in 1983, and since the late 1980s, Bon Jovi has been one of the biggest-selling acts in the world, thanks to the success of albums *Slippery When Wet* and *New Jersey*.

Brearly, David (1745–1790), **delegate** to the Constitutional Convention. Brearly attended the College of New Jersey, now known as Princeton University, near Spring Grove, his birthplace. Later, he began practicing law at Allentown, New Jersey. Brearly supported the causes of the American Revolution (1775–1783), and took part in the Constitutional Convention, where the Constitution of the United States was created. He was a member of the New Jersey Convention that **ratified** the U.S. Constitution. In 1789, President George Washington appointed him as a federal judge. He served in that position until his death in 1790.

Burr, Aaron (1756–1836), politician. Aaron Burr was born in Newark, New Jersey, in 1756. He graduated from the College of New Jersey, now Princeton University. He served as lieutenant colonel in the American Revolution (1775–1783). After practicing law in New York and serving in the state's **legislature,** Burr was elected to the U.S. **Senate** in 1791. In the

Aaron Burr

presidential election of 1800, Burr was elected vice president under Thomas Jefferson. In 1804, Burr was involved in a **duel** with Alexander Hamilton in Weehawken, New Jersey on July 11, 1804. The men faced each other with pistols, and Burr shot and killed Hamilton. Although a grand jury **indicted** Burr for murder, he was never arrested. In 1807, Burr was tried for **treason** for some questionable activities, but was found innocent. He then took up a successful law practice in New York City.

Campbell, Joseph (1817–1900), businessperson. In 1869, Joseph Campbell, a fruit merchant, formed a partnership in Camden to can tomatoes, vegetables, preserves, and other products. His soups with the familiar red and white label appeared in 1898. The company became Campbell's Soup in 1922. After World War II, the company began buying juice, frozen foods, and bakery companies, as well as several fast-food chains. It also established Campbell Soup manufacturers in several foreign countries.

Grover Cleveland

Cleveland, Grover (1837–1908), politician. Grover Cleveland was born in Caldwell, New Jersey. He was elected mayor of Buffalo, New York in 1881, and governor of New York in 1882. Cleveland is the only person to be elected U.S. president to two terms that did not directly follow each other. In 1884, Cleveland was elected the 22nd president of the United States. He was elected the 24th president in 1892. As president, Cleveland helped to rid the government of **corrupt** practices.

Cooper, James Fenimore (1789–1851), author. James Fenimore Cooper was born in Burlington, New Jersey, and raised in Cooperstown, New York. He used the setting of the New York community for his novels *The Pioneers* and *The Deerslayer*. Cooper settled in upstate New York, expecting to become a farmer. But after the success of his second novel, *The Spy*, he devoted his life to writing. Cooper is best known for his books *The Leather-Stocking Tales*, a series of five novels that describe scenes and characters of the American **frontier,** and *The Last of the Mohicans*.

Copperfield, David (b. 1956), magician. Even as a child in Metuchen, New Jersey, David Copperfield was performing **illusions** for his friends. At age 16, he was teaching magic courses at New York University. Copperfield specializes in the impossible, achieving such feats as making the Statue of Liberty disappear, **levitating** across the Grand Canyon, and escaping from Alcatraz prison in California.

Crane, Stephen (1871–1900), author. Born in Newark, New Jersey, Stephen Crane moved to New York City in 1891 to work as a newspaper writer. In his short life, Crane wrote six novels, more than 100 stories, and many newspaper articles. His best-known novel is *The Red Badge of Courage*. It is set during the Civil War (1861–1865) and tells the story of a Union soldier and his experience on the battlefield.

David Copperfield

Dinkins, David Norman (b. 1927), politician. David Dinkins was the first African-American mayor of New York City. He served as mayor from 1990 to 1994. Born in Trenton, New Jersey, Dinkins graduated from Howard University in Washington, D.C., and earned a law degree from Brooklyn Law School in 1956. Before becoming mayor, Dinkins served in the New York **legislature** for one term and as the city clerk of New York City.

Einstein, Albert (1879–1955), scientist. Albert Einstein was a German-born scientist who is thought to have one of the greatest minds of all time. He won the Nobel Prize for physics in 1921, and suggested entirely new ways of thinking about space, time, and gravitation. Einstein is probably best remembered for his theory of relativity and the equation $E = mc^2$.

Forbes, Steve (b. 1947), magazine publisher. Born in Morristown, New Jersey, Forbes graduated from Princeton University in 1970, with a degree in American history. He worked as a researcher for *Forbes* magazine, a business magazine that Forbe's grandfather founded. In 1980, he became president of Forbes Inc., which owns a variety of magazines. Then in 1990, Forbes became the editor in chief of *Forbes* magazine. Steve Forbes worked to get the Republican party nomination for U.S. president in the 1996 and 2000 elections. However, he dropped out of both races because he did not have enough support from the voters.

Steve Forbes

Ginsberg, Allen (1926–1997), poet. Allen Ginsberg grew up in Paterson, New Jersey. He was a poet of the "beat generation." Ginsberg's long and rambling poem "Howl" was first read in 1955. In the 1960s, Ginsberg and his works were well liked by the "hippies" and others who opposed the Vietnam War.

Holmes, Donald Fletcher (1910–1980), inventor. Donald Holmes was born in Woodbury, New Jersey. He graduated from college with several degrees in chemistry. Together with a partner, William Edward Hanford, he invented a way of making polyurethane, a kind of plastic. They received a **patent** for their invention in 1942.

Lange, Dorothea (1895–1965), photographer. Dorothea Lange was born in Hoboken, New Jersey, in 1895. She studied photography in college and opened a portrait studio in San Francisco in 1919. Lange is best known for her photographs of **migrant** farm families suffering during the **Great Depression.** Her realistic photographs appeared in many magazines and newspapers and helped lead the government to set up programs to help the migrant workers. After the Depression, Lange photographed life in California and other places. She traveled to places in Asia, Europe, and South America.

Dorothea Lange

Lewis, Jerry (b. 1926), comedian. Born in Newark, New Jersey, Jerry Lewis became a popular comedian during the 1940s. In 1946, he teamed up with comedian Dean Martin. Lewis is also famous for hosting the Jerry Lewis Telethon for Muscular Dystrophy.

Nicholson, Jack (b. 1937), actor and director. Jack Nicholson was born in Neptune, New Jersey. He began working in Hollywood as a messenger for a film studio. It was then that he was asked to star in his first movie. Although the movie was not successful, Nicholson received recognition for his role in a

Jack Nicholson

movie called *Easy Rider*. Other successful movies followed, and Nicholson eventually earned an Oscar for best actor for the movie *One Flew Over the Cuckoo's Nest* in 1975. Other Oscars followed for his role in *Terms of Endearment* in 1983 and for *As Good As It Gets* in 1997. In addition to acting, Jack Nicholson has also directed movies.

Shaquille O'Neal

O'Neal, Shaquille (b. 1972), athlete. Born in Newark, New Jersey, Shaquille O'Neal was raised in an army family and lived on army bases overseas. He attended college at Louisiana State University where he was a two-time All American, and was the top pick of the National Basketball Association (NBA) draft in 1992. Since then, Shaq was named Rookie of Year in 1993, was two-time NBA scoring leader in 1995 and 2000, was the regular season Most Valuable Player (MVP) in 2000, and was a three-time NBA Finals MVP in 2000, 2001, and 2002. He has also been named one of the NBA's 50 greatest players.

Paul, Alice (1885–1977), **suffragist.** Alice Paul was born in Mount Laurel, New Jersey. She was one of the first people to work for equal rights for women. She worked with British women from 1907 to 1910 to help them get the right to vote. After returning to the United States, she organized protests to push the government to grant women the right to vote. In 1913, Paul started the National American Woman Suffrage Association, an organization that worked for equal rights for women that later was known as the National Women's Party. Her efforts were rewarded when in 1920 Congress passed the 19th Amendment to the Constitution, giving women the right to vote. Paul then helped form the World Woman's Party, an international women's organization, in 1938.

Queen Latifah (b. 1970), musician and actor. Queen Latifah was born Dana Owens in East Orange, New Jersey. She is one of the most well-known female rap musicians. Queen Latifah also started an acting career, starring in several movies and receiving an Oscar nomination in 2003 for her role in the movie *Chicago*.

Queen Latifah

Robeson, Paul (1898–1976), actor, singer, and **social activist.** Robeson was born in Princeton, New Jersey, in 1898. He was a well-known singer and actor and an activist for **civil rights.** He was one of the most well-known and respected African Americans of the 1930s and 1940s. As a young man, Robeson was a good student and athlete. He received a scholarship to Rutgers College, now Rutgers University, where he earned good grades and was a star football player. Robeson went on to earn a law degree and also played professional football on weekends. Robeson performed on the stage and on radio.

Paul Robeson

He worked in many movies and was praised for his singing of black **spirituals.** In the 1930s, Robeson began working for movements for peace, **racial** equality, and better working conditions.

Scalia, Antonin (b. 1936), Supreme Court justice. Antonin Scalia was born in Trenton, New Jersey. He graduated from Georgetown University and Harvard University, with a degree in law. After holding several government positions, he was appointed as a justice to the United States Supreme Court in 1986.

Schwarzkopf, Norman (b. 1934), army general. Norman Schwarzkopf was born in Trenton, New Jersey. He graduated from the United States Military Academy in 1956 and served in the army during the Vietnam War in the 1960s. Eventually, Schwarzkopf became a general in the United States Army. He was the commander of the army in the Persian Gulf War in 1991, where more than 540,000 men and women were under his command. He retired from the army later that year.

Frank Sinatra

Sinatra, Frank (1915–1998), singer and actor. Frank Sinatra was born in Hoboken, New Jersey. He is one of the most famous singers of popular music. As a young man, Sinatra began singing with local bands. Later he began touring with a big band known as the Tommy Dorsey Band. Touring with the band made him popular, and in 1943 he began his solo singing career. In the 1940s, Sinatra also began an acting career, appearing in more than 50 movies.

Spacey, Kevin (b. 1959), actor. Kevin Spacey Fowler was born in South Orange, New Jersey, but his family moved to Los Angeles a few years later. As a child, Spacey often got into trouble. A school counselor suggested acting classes to help him use his energy. Since then, Spacey has won recognition not only for his film work but also for his television and stage performances. He is one of the most respected actors of his generation, and has earned an Oscar, a Tony, and an award as Best Actor of the Decade from England's *Empire* magazine in 1999.

Springsteen, Bruce (b. 1949), musician and songwriter. Bruce Springsteen was born and raised in Freehold, New Jersey. He started performing in the mid-1960s in small clubs on the East Coast. He signed a contract with a record company in the early 1970s, recording with the E Street Band until the 1980s, and reuniting with them again in 2002. An energetic performer, Springsteen writes nearly all the songs he performs. The words in his songs deal with the concerns and problems of average people.

Bruce Springsteen

Stone, Lucy (1818–1893), **suffragist.**
Born in Massachusetts, Lucy Stone was one of the first organizers of the women's rights movement in the United States. Although few women during her lifetime attended college, Stone attended Oberlin College, becoming one of the first women in Massachusetts to

earn a college degree, in 1847. After graduating from college, she began speaking for the **abolition** of slavery and for women's rights. In 1855, Stone married Henry Blackwell. He was a merchant and also worked for abolition. Unlike other women at the time, Stone refused to change her maiden name after her marriage. The term *Lucy Stoners* was used to refer to women who kept their own name after marriage. While living in Orange, New Jersey, Stone founded the New Jersey Woman **Suffrage** Association. She tried to vote in New Jersey, but was not allowed to do so. In 1869, Stone helped start the American Woman Suffrage Association, which worked for women's right to vote.

Meryl Streep

Streep, Meryl (b. 1949), actor. Meryl Streep was born in Summit, New Jersey. She studied acting in college and made her acting start on a stage in New York City in 1975. Streep performed in her first movie in 1977. Since that time she has made several important films, including *The Deer Hunter, Manhattan, The Hours*, and *Adaptation*. Streep is known for her skill in portraying a wide variety of characters and has earned many nominations and awards for her work.

Thomas, Dave (1932–2002), restaurateur. Dave Thomas was born in Atlantic City, New Jersey. He was adopted by a couple from Michigan when he was six months old. When he was twelve years old, Thomas got his first job at a restaurant. He is most famous for creating the Wendy's International restaurant chain. Throughout his life, Thomas also worked to promote the adoption of foster children.

Travolta, John (b. 1954), actor. John Travolta was born in Englewood, New Jersey, the youngest of six children. All but one member of Travolta's family was in show business. Travolta found fame in the 1970s with hits in films, on television, and on the

Dave Thomas

radio. He was the star of the television show *Welcome Back, Kotter,* and found success in the movies *Saturday Night Fever* and *Grease*. His career slowed in the 1980s, but beginning in the early 1990s, Travolta found the spotlight again. He has since starred in several films, including *Pulp Fiction, Phenomenon, Face/Off,* and *The General's Daughter.*

John Travolta

Whitman, Walt (1819– 1892), poet. Although born in New York, Whitman spent the last years of his life in Camden, New Jersey. Whitman's *Leaves of Grass*, a book of poems, is thought to be one of the world's most important works of literature. Many of Whitman's poems praise the United States and the ideas of **democracy.** He continued to write poems until his death.

Williams, William Carlos (1883–1963), physician and writer. William Carlos Williams was born in Rutherford. After receiving a medical degree from the University of Pennsylvania in 1906 and studying in Leipzig, Germany, he spent the rest of his life in Rutherford, practicing medicine and writing. He wrote stories, plays, and autobiographies, as well as poems. His most memorable achievement is probably his five books of poetry about the New Jersey city of Paterson.

Woodrow Wilson

Wilson, Woodrow (1856-1924), politician. Woodrow was born in Staunton, Virginia. In 1875, he started his college education at Princeton University. He served as president of the University before being elected governor of New Jersey in 1910. As governor, Wilson worked to bring **reforms** to New Jersey. His reforms drew national attention, and in 1912, he ran for president of the United States. He became the 28th president and served two terms.

Map of New Jersey

0   20 mi.

New York

Pennsylvania

New Jersey

Atlantic
Ocean

Delaware

Delaware River

Lake
Hopatcong

S. Branch Raritan River

N. Branch Raritan River

Passaic

Mahwah

Hackensack

Wayne
Paterson

Paramus
Teaneck
Fort Lee

West Orange
Livingston

North Bergen

Morristown

Hoboken

Newark

Jersey City

Elizabeth

Bayonne

Piscataway
Edison

Plainfield

New Brunswick

Perth Amboy

Sandy Hook

Matawan
Holmdel

Red Bank

Princeton

Long Branch

Ewing

✪ Trenton

Asbury Park

Toms River

Willingboro

Browns Mills

Lakehurst

Camden

Point Pleasant

Cherry Hill
Haddonfield

Delaware River

Marlton

Barnegat

Long Beach
Island

Vineland

Millville

ATLANTIC
OCEAN

Atlantic City

Ocean City
Avalon

Villas

Cape May

Glossary

abolition ban slavery. A person who wants slavery banned is an abolitionist.

ancestor one from whom an individual has descended

apprentice person who is learning a trade or art by experience under a skilled worker

canal artificial waterway for boats

census count of population and the gathering of information about that population

civil rights rights of personal liberty guaranteed by the U.S. Constitution

climate weather conditions that are usual for a certain area

colony distant territory under the control of a nation. People who settled in a colony were colonists.

Continental Army American soldiers in the American Revolution

corrupt lacking honesty

culture ideas, skills, arts, and a way of life of a certain people at a certain time

debt something owed to another

delegate person sent to a meeting to represent a community

democracy government that is run by the people

density amount of something in a specific area

descent to be born of; to come from a given source

diverse having variety

duel combat between two persons fought with deadly weapons and with witnesses present

ethnic belonging to a group with a particular culture

famine time when food is scarce and people are starving

fertile bearing crops or vegetation in abundance

fort strong building used for defense against enemy attack

fortified made strong

frontier edge of a settled part of a country

Great Depression economic collapse in 1929, in which unemployment was high and many businesses failed

Great Migration movement of African Americans from the southern United States to the North

heritage something that comes from one's ancestors

illusion misleading image presented to the eye

immigrant one who moves to another country to settle

independence not being controlled by someone or something else

indicted to charge with an offense or crime

industry group of businesses that offer a similar product or service

inhumanity cruel act or attitude

legislature governmental body that makes and changes laws

levitating rising or floating in the air especially in seeming to go against gravity

massacre violent and cruel killing of many people

metropolitan area surrounding a large city

migrant person who moves from place to place

migrate to move from one place to another for food or to breed

militia citizens with minimal training who are called into military duty during emergencies

municipality town or city having its own local government

natural resource something from nature that is available to take care of a need

ore rock or mineral from which a metal can be obtained

Parliament assembly that is the highest legislative body of the United Kingdom

patent protected by a document that gives the inventor of something the only right to make, use, and sell the invention for a certain number of years

persecute treat badly

racial of, relating to, or based on race

racism unfair treatment of a person based on race

ratified gave legal approval

reform to make better and improve faults

reservation public land set aside for use by Native Americans

resign to give up an office by a formal or official act

revitalize give new life to

rural having to do with the country or farmland

Senate upper and smaller branch of a legislature in the United States

social activist someone who publicly supports a cause

spiritual religious folk song developed especially by African Americans of the southern United States

suburb city or town just outside a larger city

suffragist someone who fought for the right to vote

thrive to do very well

trade (n.) work in which a person takes part regularly

trade (v.) buying and selling of goods

treason crime of trying to overthrow the government

treaty agreement between two parties

urban relating to the city

More Books to Read

Kummer, Patricia K. *New Jersey*. Minnetonka, Minn.: Bridgestone Books, 1998.

Moragne, Wendy. *New Jersey*. Tarrytown, N.Y.: Benchmark Books, 2000.

Scholl, Elizabeth. *New Jersey*. San Francisco: Children's Book Press, 2002.

Stein, R. Conrad and Deborah Ken. *New Jersey*. Danbury, Conn.: Children's Press, 1998.

Welsbacher, Anne. *New Jersey*. Edina, Minn.: Checkerboard Library, 1998.

Index

About the Author

Mark Stewart makes his home in New Jersey. A graduate of Duke University with a degree in history, Stewart has authored more than 100 nonfiction titles for the school and library market. He and his wife Sarah have two daughters, Mariah and Rachel.